ANCIEN[T]

SOCIAL MEDIA IN THE AGE OF SOCRATES

Martin Gitlin

45th Parallel Press

Published in the United States of America by Cherry Lake Publishing Group
Ann Arbor, Michigan
www.cherrylakepublishing.com

Reading Adviser: Beth Walker Gambro, MS, Ed., Reading Consultant, Yorkville, IL

Photo Credits: © Preto Perola /Shutterstock, cover, title page; © ZU_09/iStock.com, 4; © Katoosha/Shutterstock, 7; © Barbarajo/Shutterstock, 8; © krechet/Shutterstock, 12; © Constantinos Iliopoulos/Shutterstock, 14; © Panos Karas/Shutterstock, 16; George E. Koronaios, CC BY-SA 4.0 via Wikimedia Commons, 18; © ShutterOK/Shutterstock, 20; © Michael Avory/Shutterstock, 23; © Oleg Golovnev/Shutterstock, 24; © Angelo Cordeschi/Shutterstock, 27; © RPBaiao/Shutterstock, 28; Unknown Chinese artist, Public domain, via Wikimedia Commons, 29

Graphic Element Credits: Graphic Element Credits: Cover, multiple interior pages: © Andrey_Kuzmin/Shutterstock, © cajoer/Shutterstock, © GUSAK OLENA/Shutterstock, © Eky Studio/Shutterstock

Copyright © 2025 by Cherry Lake Publishing Group
All rights reserved. No part of this book may be reproduced or utilized
in any form or by any means without written permission from the publisher.
45TH Parallel Press is an imprint of Cherry Lake Publishing Group.

Library of Congress Cataloging-in-Publication Data has been filed and is available at catalog.loc.gov.

Cherry Lake Publishing Group would like to acknowledge the work of the Partnership for 21st Century Learning, a Network of Battelle for Kids. Please visit http://www.battelleforkids.org/networks/p21 for more information.

Printed in the United States of America

Note from publisher: Websites change regularly, and their future contents are outside of our control.
Supervise children when conducting any recommended online searches for extended learning opportunities.

About the Author
Martin Gitlin is an educational book author based in Connecticut. He won more than 45 awards as a newspaper journalist from 1991 to 2002. Included was a first-place award from the Associated Press. That organization voted him as one of the top four feature writers in Ohio in 2002. Martin has had about 250 books published since 2006. Most of them were written for students. He has authored many books about history.

TABLE OF CONTENTS

Introduction 4

Chapter 1: Athens Agora 8

Chapter 2: Seeds of Democracy 12

Chapter 3: The Great Greeks 16

Chapter 4: The Roman Forum 20

Chapter 5: Ancient Plays 24

Chapter 6: Dangerous Dinner in China 28

Glossary 32
Learn More 32
Index 32

INTRODUCTION

Pharaohs ruled ancient Egypt. They had mail. They used couriers. Couriers sent notices to people.

Imagine no phones. No emails. No texts. Imagine talking as the only communication. Most of human history relied on talking. Talking was done in person.

People had ideas. They wanted to talk about life. They wanted to talk about their countries. They wanted to talk about their families. They wanted to share opinions. They wanted to meet others. So they met. They gathered. They spoke to one another. They talked in public places. They discussed issues. They voted on ideas. They elected leaders.

Talking to others was important. Ancient people often had little power. They banded together. They met at public **forums**. Forums are gathering places.

Times have changed. Technology created tools. People use phones. They use computers. The internet created new ways of talking. Today, people connect online. They're on social media. They're on discussion boards. They email. They post. They direct message. They comment.

People also meet in real life. They like being with others. They share entertainment. They attend sporting events. They go to concerts. They hike. They eat. They can do all kinds of activities.

People are social. They share ideas. They hold meetings. They talk about issues. They plan things. They create change. It was the same in ancient times.

Ancient Chinese shadow puppetry was a way stories were told for entertainment.

CHAPTER ONE

A court voted to renovate a railway line. This line was built through the Athens Agora. This happened in 2011. Some Greeks got angry.

Athens Agora

It was first a graveyard. The site was full of **tombs**. This was in 1600 BCE. A thousand years passed. By 600 BCE, it came to life. It was the **Agora** of Athens. An agora is a public open space. It's a meeting place. Today, Athens is the capital of Greece. Back then, it was its own nation.

People say that Socrates spoke at the agora. Socrates asked questions. He did this to teach. He was a philosopher. A playwright heard him. He burned his plays. He became a philosopher too. He was Plato. He wrote about Socrates. Socrates changed his life. Socrates was an ancient influencer.

The agora was more than a meeting spot. People worshipped Greek gods there. They also shopped there. They bought food. They bought art. They traded. Ideas spread to other lands.

The agora was busy with life. Sellers sold goods from benches or tents. People drove ox carts. Others met under shady trees. They spoke. They shared opinions. Sailors told stories. They bragged about their voyages. Farmers talked about their crops. **Philosophers** discussed the meaning of life. Philosophers are thinkers.

Everyone waited for a special festival. All of Athens was invited. It happened each year. It celebrated Athena. She is an ancient Greek goddess. People marched from the agora to the Acropolis. The Acropolis is an ancient **citadel**. A citadel is a fortress. Important worship happened there. Important politics happened there.

The agora was important to the Greeks. Persians attacked in 480 BCE. They destroyed some of the agora. So the Greeks rebuilt it. The new agora was bigger and better. There were new buildings. There were new fountains. There were new temples. The agora was important for hundreds of years.

ANCIENT RULES

Ancient Rome had a public space too. It was the Roman Forum. Women were allowed in the Roman Forum. But men had the most important roles. Not all women had freedom. It depended on their wealth. It depended on their social status.

Rich women had businesses. They sold goods at the forum. Others were hairdressers. A few were doctors. There were many ancient Roman women who were slaves. Some did manual labor. They cleaned and did farm work.

Women usually stayed home. They wove thread into cloth. They cooked meals. They couldn't vote. They couldn't run for office. Women usually had only one way to exert power. They influenced husbands. They influenced male relatives.

CHAPTER TWO

The Temple of Hephaestus stands on a hill looking over the ancient agora in Athens, Greece.

Seeds of Democracy

Greek democracy may have started in the agora. **Democracy** is government by the people. The word *democracy* comes from Greece. It comes from 2 Greek words. One is *demos*. That means "people." The other is *kratos*. That means "rule." So *democracy* means "people rule."

The Greeks were active in politics. Voting was important to them. Many Greeks were elected to government. Elections were important. They let voters choose their leaders. Elections included a peaceful transfer of power. But that isn't true in some countries today.

Democracy has changed in modern times. Not everyone has to contribute. All Greek citizens did. People had to play active roles in government. Those who didn't were fined.

There was another big difference. In Athens's democracy, Greek women and slaves were excluded. They weren't counted as citizens. They couldn't vote. Children were also not citizens.

Athens had a special system. Five hundred people were chosen every year. They had to serve in the government. They made new laws. People voted on each law. It was called direct democracy.

Voting in ancient Greece first took place at the Athens agora. Then it was moved to a hill called the Pnyx. This was near the Acropolis.

A NICE STORY

Poor people needed help in ancient Rome. They struggled to buy food. They needed clothing. They had to pay for land. Such problems still exist for people today.

The Roman emperor Nerva did something about it. He ruled from 96 to 98 CE. Nerva began a **welfare** program called *alimenta*. Welfare means well-being. Nerva's program provided money for orphans. It also helped other poor children. Emperor Trajan expanded the program. He taxed landowners. This forced the wealthy to help. The program ended around 272 CE. That was during the rule of Emperor Aurelian.

CHAPTER THREE

Aristotle's ideas developed sciences. Examples are zoology and physics.

The Great Greeks

People both talked and listened at the Athens Agora. They all learned. They discussed philosophy. They debated the meaning of life. Scientific **theory** was born. Theories are ideas. They explain facts or events.

Great minds gathered at the agora. Socrates was a great Greek thinker. He questioned common beliefs. He believed in debate. Debating was a means to gain wisdom. Among his students was Plato. Plato spoke about social structure. He believed in 3 classes of **society**. One was those who governed. The second was the warriors. The third was workers.

Aristotle learned from Plato. Then he taught others. He spoke at food stalls. He talked near fountains. He made a huge impact on science.

Hippocrates taught in his local agora. He's the father of modern medicine. He believed in **ethical** treatment. Ethical means fair and honest. Ethics was the basis of his Hippocratic Oath. Many medical students still take the oath. They vow to help people. They vow to do no harm.

Another great Greek was Pythagoras. Pythagoras studied math. He helped found **geometry**. Geometry is the study of shapes, sizes, and angles.

Many influencers in the agora held classes there. They shared their ideas. They taught them to others.

Some doubt Hippocrates created the Hippocratic oath. Its origin is not known for sure.

MYSTERY SOLVED OR UNSOLVED?

Archaeologists study human history. They found something awful in Greece. This happened in the 1930s. They were digging at an ancient Athens Agora site. They found 450 human skeletons. All were discovered in a well. Many were infants.

How did the infants die? Two ideas arose. One was murder. The other was a **plague**. Further research was done. It turned out neither was true. The infants' skulls were studied. About 1 out of 3 died from **meningitis**. Meningitis affects the brain and spine. The others died from other sicknesses. Very few lived more than a week.

Newborns often died in ancient times. But diggers rarely find their remains. Some were buried under floors. Others didn't get burials. The Greeks didn't see them as complete people.

CHAPTER FOUR

Today, the Roman Forum attracts 4.5 million tourists per year.

The Roman Forum

It was 753 BCE. A legend centers on that year. It's about twin brothers. Their names are Remus and Romulus. It's said Romulus killed Remus. Then he declared himself king. He named Rome after himself.

That story has been debated. But one thing is certain. The Roman **Republic** gave birth to the Roman Forum. A republic is a form of government. People elect their leaders. It is a type of democracy.

The forum began as a market. People shopped there. Then it expanded. It became a meeting place. It continued to grow. Statues were built. Arches were built. Other buildings were built.

The forum became the heart of Rome. People gathered. They discussed politics. They discussed social issues.

They debated their views. This helped Romans understand each other. But the forum did more. It changed society.

The forum hosted events. Some events were small. People gave speeches there. They threw parties. They held business meetings. They sold goods. Students took classes there. They learned all types of topics.

Some forum events were big. Elections were held there. Criminal trials took place there. Fans packed the forum for **gladiator** matches. Gladiators are warriors. Some fought to the death.

The forum had many buildings. One was the Temple of Saturn. It was dedicated to Saturn. Saturn was the god of farming. The rostrum was a platform for speakers. Speakers shouted opinions on many subjects.

The Senate House was also known as the Curia. It was turned into a church. This happened in 630 BCE.

CHAPTER FIVE

Greek theater had rules. The death of a character wasn't allowed to be seen onstage. It could only be heard offstage.

Ancient Plays

Ancient people did not gather just to talk. They wanted to be entertained. They watched plays. They loved the theater.

Theater began with the Greeks. First came the **tragedies**. Tragedies are dramas. They're sad. They were written by famous playwrights. Among them were Sophocles and Aristophanes. These plays were performed in open theaters. Most were inspired by Greek myths. The characters often dealt with **moral** issues. Moral refers to being right or wrong. Audiences understood these stories. They had moral problems in their own lives.

Ancient Greeks also enjoyed **comedies**. Comedies are funny. They had singing. They had dancing. Actors wore wild costumes. They made people laugh. That was needed. Ancient people had tough lives. Laughter made them feel better.

Crowds of thousands attended plays. Ancient Romans jammed into the Theater of Pompey. That was Rome's first permanent theater. It opened in 55 BCE.

Romans also produced tragedies and comedies. Actors dressed in Greek costumes. But Romans had different tastes. They liked grand performances. They preferred gladiator fights. They preferred **mock** sea battles. Mock means pretend.

Plays became part of huge festivals. They rarely dealt with serious issues. Great minds did not attend. They turned to other types of performers. Among them were **mimes**. Mimes are silent masked characters. They told stories with movements. They made hand gestures. They also danced.

The Theater of Pompey was dedicated by Pompey the Great. Pompey was a military leader.

27

CHAPTER SIX

The Qin Dynasty of China lasted just 15 years after the Zhou Dynasty. The Zhou Dynasty lasted 789 years.

Dangerous Dinner in China

Not all ancient gatherings were friendly. One in China was not. It was the Hongmen **Banquet**. Banquets are fancy dinners or festivals. People gather to share ideas. They make friends. The Hongmen Banquet occurred in Xianyang. That was a capital city in the Qin **Dynasty**. Dynasties are ruling families.

It was 206 BCE. The event was supposed to be festive. Two enemies showed up. They almost made it deadly. They were Liu Bang and Xiang Yu. Liu had conquered the city. He planned to declare himself king. Xiang wanted the throne for himself. He had an advisor named Fan Zeng. Fan told Xiang to murder Liu. So Xiang invited Liu to the banquet. Liu accepted. Both men brought soldiers with them. All seemed well at first. Liu treated Xiang with respect. That pleased the host. He didn't want to kill Liu. But Fan had different ideas.

Fan still wanted Liu gone. He turned to a banquet entertainer. Fan asked him to kill Liu. This would look like part of the performance.

That is when Xiang Bo stepped in. He was the uncle of Xiang Yu. He was also a friend of Liu. Xiang Bo sensed danger. He blocked every sword attack. Then Fan Kuai burst into the room. Fan Kuai was Liu's general. He was dressed in armor. He carried a sword. Fan Kuai glared at Xiang. He scolded Xiang for trying to kill Liu.

Xiang let Liu go. He got away on a horse. Their armies fought at the Battle of Gaixia. Xiang lost badly. He then killed himself.

Liu Bang won the Battle of Gaixia. This launched the Han Dynasty. It made him emperor.

VERY IMPORTANT PEOPLE

Who wrote the first Greek tragedies? It was Aeschylus. He was born in 525 BCE. He wrote his first plays in 498 BCE. He was also a military hero. He fought the Persians. He helped Greece win. That was about 490 BCE.

Little is known about Aeschylus. But his play *The Persians* is famous. It described the Persian defeat. It was told from the Persian side. It was paid for by Pericles. Pericles was a Greek general. He was a politician. The play was a huge success in Athens.

Aeschylus wrote nearly 90 plays. But only 7 are known. His tomb mentions his military service. It does not mention his plays.

GLOSSARY

agora (AA-guh-ruh) in ancient Greece, a public open space used for assemblies and markets

archaeologists (ar-kee-AH-luh-jists) scientists who study ancient ruins and objects

banquet (BAYNG-kwuht) a fancy dinner or festival

citadel (SIH-tuh-duhl) a fortress over a city

comedies (KAH-muh-deez) funny plays with happy endings

democracy (di-MAH-kruh-see) a system of government in which people elect their representatives and help make decisions

dynasty (DIYE-nuh-stee) a ruling family

ethical (E-thih-kuhl) morally justified

forums (FOR-uhmz) gathering places for meetings and other activities

gladiator (GLA-dee-ay-tur) an ancient Roman who fought animals and other men

meningitis (me-nuhn-JIE-tuhs) inflammation of the brain membranes

mimes (MIEMZ) entertainers who tell stories only through gestures

mock (MAWK) to copy or pretend or fake

moral (MOHR-uhl) of or relating to the judgment of right and wrong

philosophers (fah-LAH-suh-ferz) people who seek wisdom

plague (PLAYG) an infectious disease that kills many people

republic (ri-PUH-blik) a form of government in which the people elect, or choose, their leaders

society (suh-SIE-uh-tee) a community of people

theory (THEE-uh-ree) an idea or set of ideas that is intended to explain facts or events

tombs (TOOMZ) graves or places where dead people are buried

tragedies (TRAH-juh-deez) plays dealing with tragic or sad events and having unhappy endings

welfare (WEL-fare) public or private aid for people in need

LEARN MORE

Fet, Catherine. *Ancient Rome for Kids Through the Lives of its Heroes, Emperors, and Philosophers.* Independently Published, 2020.

Universal Politics. *What Is Democracy? Ancient Greece's Legacy/Systems of Government.* Universal Politics, 2019.

Search online with an adult:
Kids Love Greece: Play and Learn in Ancient Agora for Kids.

INDEX

Aeschylus, 31
Agora of Athens, 8–10, 12, 13, 14, 16, 18, 19
Aristotle, 16, 17
arts and entertainment, 7, 22, 24–27, 31
Athens, 8–10, 12–14, 16, 18, 19, 31
burials, 19
China, 7, 28–30
democracy, 13–14
discourse, 4, 5–6, 9, 10, 17, 18, 21–22

diseases, 19
drama, 7, 24–27, 31
dynasties, China, 28–30
forums, 5, 9–10, 11, 20–23
governments, 13–14, 21–22
Greece, 8–10, 12–14, 16–19, 24–27, 31
Hippocrates, 18
Hongmen Banquet (China), 29–30
infants and children, 14, 15, 19

Liu Bang, 29–30
medicine, 18, 19
Nerva (emperor), 15
philosophers, 10, 16–18
poverty, 15
Pythagoras, 18
Roman Forum, 11, 20–23
Rome, 11, 15, 20–22, 26, 27
sciences, 16, 17, 18
social status, 11, 14, 15, 17

storytelling, 7, 10, 24–26, 31
theater, 7, 24–27, 31
trade, 10–11, 21, 22
welfare, 15
women's rights, 11, 14
Xiang Yu, 29–30